Seymour Public Library
46 Church Street
Seymour, CT 06483

Conquering Disease

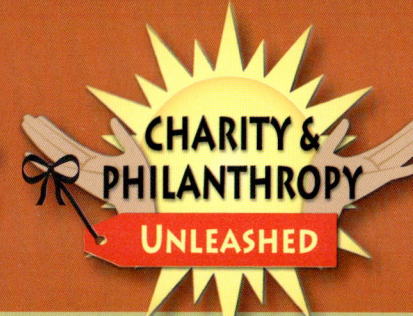
CHARITY & PHILANTHROPY UNLEASHED

Marylou Morano Kjelle

Mitchell Lane
PUBLISHERS
P.O. Box 196
Hockessin, DE 19707

J
362.1
KJEL

Conquering Disease
Emergency Aid
Environmental Protection
Helping Children with Life-Threatening Medical Issues
Helping Our Veterans
Preserving Human Rights Around the World
The Quest to End World Hunger
Support for Education

Copyright © 2015 by Mitchell Lane Publishers

All rights reserved. No part of this book may be reproduced without written permission from the publisher. Printed and bound in the United States of America.

PUBLISHER'S NOTE: The facts in this book have been thoroughly researched. Documentation of such research can be found on pages 44–45. While every possible effort has been made to ensure accuracy, the publisher will not assume liability for damages caused by inaccuracies in the data, and makes no warranty on the accuracy of the information contained herein.

The Internet sites referenced herein were active as of the publication date. Due to the fleeting nature of some web sites, we cannot guarantee that they will all be active when you are reading this book.

Printing 1 2 3 4 5 6 7 8 9

Library of Congress
Cataloging-in-Publication Data
Kjelle, Marylou Morano.
  Conquering disease / Marylou Morano Kjelle.
    pages cm. — (Charity and philanthropy unleashed)
  Audience: Age 9–13.
  Audience: Grade 4–8.
  Includes bibliographical references and index.
  ISBN 978-1-61228-576-4 (library bound)
 1. Medical policy—United States—Juvenile literature. 2. Medicine—Research—United States—Juvenile literature. 3. Medicine, Preventive—United States—Juvenile literature. I. Title.
  RA395.A3K56 2015
  362.1—dc23
                                            2014006921
eBook ISBN: 9781612286143

PBP

Contents

Introduction 4
CHAPTER 1
　CONQUERING CHILDHOOD DISEASES 6
　　The GAVI Alliance 13
CHAPTER 2
　CONQUERING CANCER 14
　　What is Cancer? 21
CHAPTER 3
　CONQUERING COMMUNICABLE DISEASES 22
　　Conquering AIDS 29
CHAPTER 4
　BIG STEPS FORWARD 30
　　Conquering Smallpox 37
CHAPTER 5
　YOU CAN HELP, TOO! 38
　　Conquering Disease 41
What You Can Do to Help 42
Chapter Notes 43
Further Reading 44
　Books 44
　On the Internet 44
　Works Consulted 44
Glossary 45
Index 47

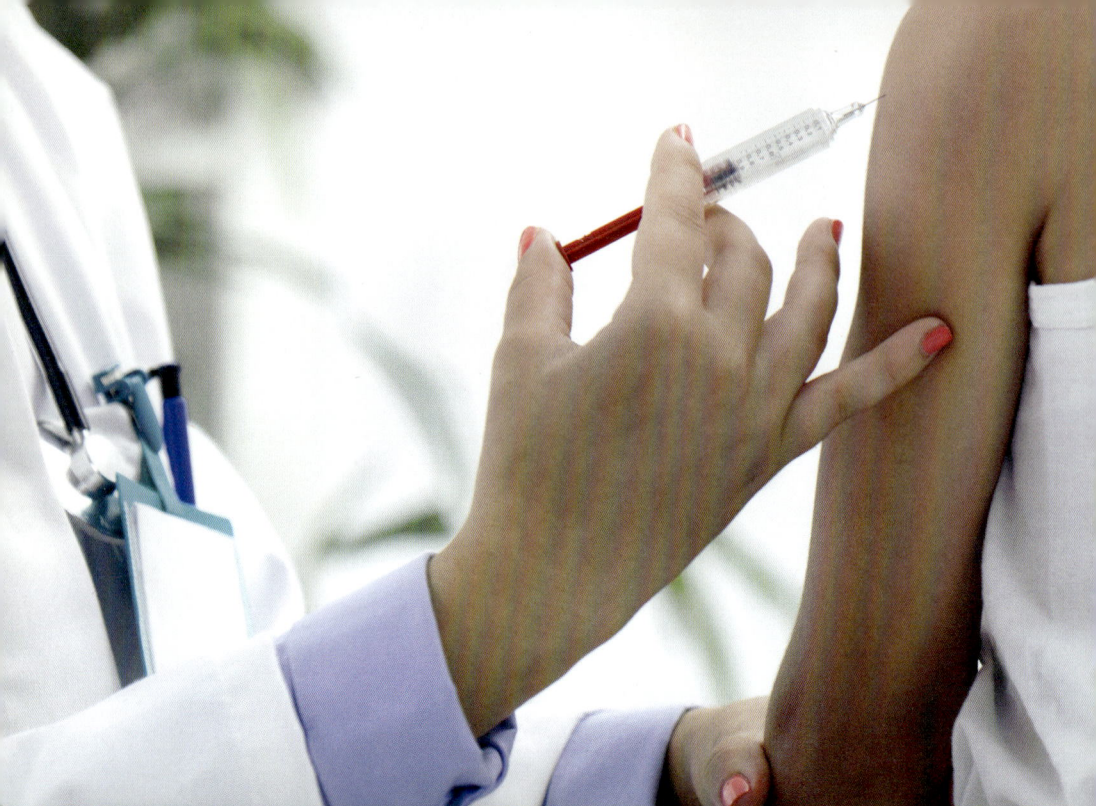

Introduction

Early people did not understand disease. They didn't know what caused it, or how to prevent it. They didn't understand how to make themselves better when they became sick, and often the disease killed them. Lacking knowledge about health and sickness, primitive people came up with their own explanations for disease.

Some believed disease was caused when evil spirits entered the body. Others thought magical spells caused disease. Later, people sought to connect disease to religion. According to their beliefs, disease was the result of making God angry.

Fast-forward thousands of years to the twenty-first century. We know a lot more about disease today. We know humans are susceptible to thousands of diseases, and that each is caused not by magic or evil spells, but by one of many causes, such as exposure to a virus or toxin. We know that some diseases can be prevented, and some can be cured. We have medicines and other

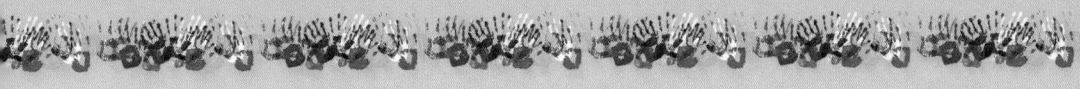

ways of treating disease, but new medical discoveries and breakthroughs are still needed. We are on the road to conquering disease, but we have a long way to go.

Conducting research, building sanitation systems, and caring for the sick are tasks that are all needed in order to conquer disease. However, huge sums of money are also needed to complete these projects. Some governments, especially those of less industrialized, developing countries, don't have the money to do all it takes to fight the diseases that affect their populations. Increasingly, philanthropies and charitable organizations are making a difference in the effort to conquer disease. A philanthropy is a humanitarian organization dedicated to helping others. They are neutral organizations that do not get involved in the politics of the countries they work in; their goal is to help people. A philanthropy is not a business; it is not striving for financial gain, like a corporation. Therefore, a philanthropy is often referred to as a nonprofit organization. And since it isn't part of a government, a philanthropy is also called a non-governmental organization (NGO). Sometimes a philanthropy is called a foundation. This is because its resources are the basis, or foundation, of the charitable work it does. There are thousands, possibly even millions, of philanthropies at work throughout the world.

Philanthropies are helping to conquer disease in many ways. They fund the research of investigators who are studying disease prevention and searching for cures. They develop programs to help those already afflicted with a disease enjoy a better quality of life. Many philanthropies work in developing countries where people have few governmental services. There philanthropic volunteers build and start up sanitation systems and show people how to grow nutritious food, two things that are necessary if disease is to be conquered. And philanthropies send doctors and other healthcare workers all over the world to teach people how to get and stay healthy by practicing good hygiene and preventing disease with vaccinations. The war against disease needs to be fought on many fronts. Philanthropies are a mighty army in this war. With their help, we are working toward the day when disease will be completely eliminated.

CHAPTER 1
Conquering Childhood Diseases

If you were born in 1900, odds are you would have died before you turned fifty years old. You might not have even survived your childhood. Back then, almost 15 percent of all babies born in the United States died before they turned one year old. If you made it to your first birthday, there was still a good chance you would not make it to age fifteen. You might have gotten pneumonia, measles, cholera, or diphtheria. In the early 1900s, these four diseases together killed more young children than any other.[1] In addition to contagious diseases, children often died from drinking contaminated water and unpasteurized milk, eating food that had little nutrition, or living in unsanitary conditions.[2]

Disease still exists, but it doesn't threaten us the way it once did. Today, vaccines prevent many of the diseases that afflicted children, as well as adults, in the past. Antibiotics and other powerful medications are routinely used to treat and cure other diseases. Tests are now available that allow doctors to detect disease early, when it is easier to treat and cure. Many of these medical accomplishments are due, at least in part, to the work of philanthropies.

From Disaster Relief to Measles Vaccines

The American Red Cross was formed by Clara Barton in Washington, DC. Clara had been a war nurse during the American Civil War (1861–1865) where she had witnessed the suffering of wounded soldiers. After the war, she helped soldiers' families find their loved ones, both living and dead. Clara's wartime

Clara Barton was a compassionate woman who served as a nurse in the Civil War. Her concern and empathy for the soldiers earned her the nickname, "the angel of the battlefield." After the war, Clara continued to serve others by founding the American Red Cross.

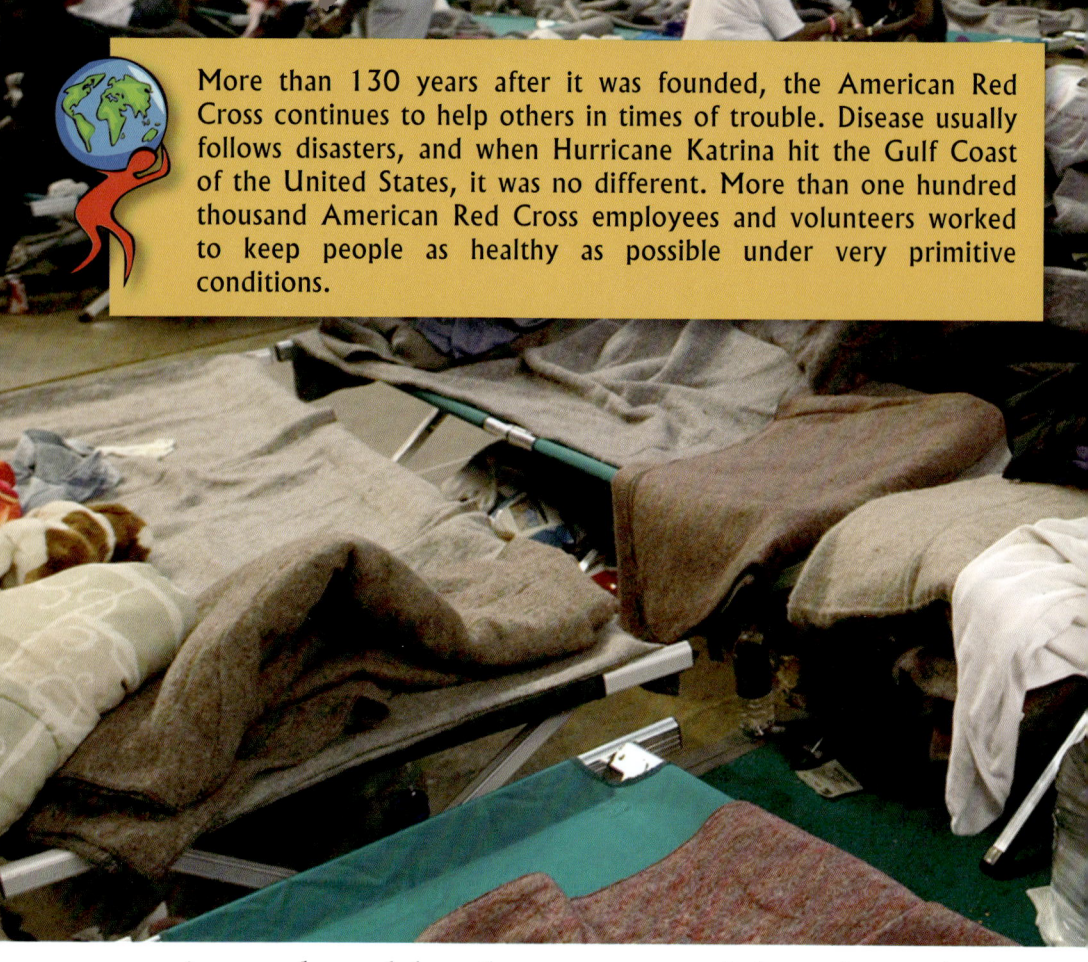

More than 130 years after it was founded, the American Red Cross continues to help others in times of trouble. Disease usually follows disasters, and when Hurricane Katrina hit the Gulf Coast of the United States, it was no different. More than one hundred thousand American Red Cross employees and volunteers worked to keep people as healthy as possible under very primitive conditions.

experiences showed her there was a need for a humanitarian organization that could help people not only during war, but in peacetime as well. In 1881 Clara brought the International Red Cross movement, which had started in Switzerland, to the United States. Under Clara's guidance, the American Red Cross grew from providing wartime assistance in the United States to helping with disaster relief throughout the world.

Over its 130-year history, the Red Cross name has come to symbolize assistance during national and international disasters. For example, on December 26, 2004, an earthquake with a 9.0 magnitude under the Indian Ocean caused a massive tsunami that killed 230,000 people in fourteen countries. The American Red Cross joined other humanitarian organizations in offering relief to the survivors. Disease usually follows disasters of this magnitude. To head off an epidemic, more than 14,400 volunteers were trained in community-based health care and first aid.[3] Eight months later, in late August 2005, Hurricane Katrina stormed the Gulf Coast of the United States, inflicting damage to eleven states. To meet the needs of the victims of this disaster, the organization launched its largest relief effort to date. Working as a partner with other organizations, the American Red Cross's Hurricane Recovery Program rebuilt homes damaged by the storm, and provided health services to those who were affected.[4]

Recently, the American Red Cross has begun to take an active role in the fight against a childhood disease called measles. In 2001, the American Red Cross joined the Centers for Disease Control (CDC), the United Nations Children's Fund (UNICEF), the World Health Organization (WHO), and the United Nations Foundation in a global Measles and Rubella Initiative. The goal of this program is to eradicate measles throughout the world. Measles, a contagious infection of the respiratory system, is caused by a virus. The symptoms are runny nose, fever, and

Chapter 1

cough. Measles also causes small bumps to form over a flat red skin rash. Measles can sometimes lead to ear infections and pneumonia. The disease is spread when an infected person coughs or sneezes.

Rubella, or German measles, is also caused by a virus. The symptoms of rubella are not as serious as those of measles, although if a pregnant woman is exposed to rubella, the baby may be born with congenital rubella syndrome. This condition can cause heart problems, hearing and vision loss, and intellectual problems in the child.[5]

Measles and rubella are uncommon in industrialized countries where most children receive an MMR (mumps, measles, and rubella) vaccine by the time they are eighteen months old. Children who live in developing countries, however, are at great risk of catching measles and dying from it. According to the Measles and Rubella Initiative, eighteen children die from measles every hour. The goal of the Initiative is to reduce worldwide deaths from measles by 95 percent by or before the year 2015.[6] In one decade, over 1.1 billion vaccinations have been provided to children in eighty countries, many with help from the Initiative. Still, there is much work to be done. Dr. Myrna Charles of the American Red Cross said, "[In 2013], measles and rubella outbreaks are occurring in many areas of the world where people [are not vaccinated against] these viruses."[7] Many philanthropic workers are striving to bring vaccinations to the people who need them. Their job also includes educating people about disease and how it is spread. The Measles and Rubella Initiative works throughout the world, wherever there are unvaccinated children. Some countries that the Initiative has recently worked in are the United Kingdom, Nigeria, Pakistan, and Syria.[8]

A Billionaire's Compassion Circles the Globe

In addition to the Measles and Rubella Initiative, other philanthropies are helping to vaccinate the children of the world against childhood illnesses. The Bill & Melinda Gates Foundation

CONQUERING CHILDHOOD DISEASES

Measles was once a common disease, but thanks to the measles vaccine, it is now rarely seen in developed countries like the United States. When the disease does strike, it starts with a fever, then progresses to a runny nose. Finally, a rash of red spots breaks out over the entire body.

is one. In the 1990s, Bill Gates, one of the founders of Microsoft, and his wife, Melinda, realized that there were millions of children throughout the world who needed simple medical treatments. Many of these children were dying from diseases that had been eliminated in the United States long ago. In 2000 the Gates family formed the Bill & Melinda Gates Foundation. One of their first projects, which continues today, is to work to meet the eight Millennium Development Goals established by the United Nations, by joining with other philanthropic organizations. These global goals are intended to improve the quality of life of

The chairman and co-founder of Microsoft, Bill Gates, and his wife Melinda visit the Manhiça Health Research Center in Mozambique. Through their foundation, the Gates family is committed to wiping out malaria and other diseases that attack children in poor, undeveloped countries where health care is limited.

people living in developing countries by the year 2015. One of the goals is to combat disease.

Some of the projects the Bill & Melinda Gates Foundation has contributed to are HIV/AIDS prevention in India, research to develop a vaccine for malaria, and the elimination of poliomyelitis, an infectious disease caused by a virus that affects the muscles. The Foundation is also committed to the elimination of tuberculosis (TB), a highly contagious disease of the lungs caused by a bacterium. TB is spread by inhalation. When someone who has TB coughs or sneezes, droplets containing the bacteria are released into the air. Inhaling air with TB droplets puts a person at risk of contracting the disease. Funding from the Gates Foundation is allowing scientists to research ways to conquer TB. The researchers are investigating new drugs, diagnostic tests, and a vaccine.[9]

The GAVI Alliance

In 2000, the Bill & Melinda Gates Foundation helped to form the Global Alliance for Vaccines and Immunization (now called the GAVI Alliance), a partnership between WHO, UNICEF, the World Bank, national governments, and corporations to vaccinate people throughout the world against all preventable diseases. According to WHO estimates, more than 370 million children had received one or more vaccines from GAVI by the end of 2012. This includes 46 million children vaccinated in 2012 alone. Countries are eligible to receive immunizations from GAVI based on economic status.[10] GAVI believes it can prevent almost 4 million future deaths by immunizing 243 million children from 2011–2015. One of GAVI's most-used vaccines is the pentavalent vaccine. This is a five-in-one vaccine that immunizes against diphtheria, tetanus, pertussis, hepatitis B, and HIB. Caused by viruses and bacteria, these diseases are all potentially deadly, especially in children. Additional vaccines administered by GAVI act against yellow fever, pneumonia, meningitis, and other diseases. "Our job will not be complete until every boy and every girl in the developing world can be confidently called 'a fully immunized child,'" said Seth Berkley, MD, the Chief Executive Officer (CEO) of the GAVI Alliance.[11]

GAVI's mission is to save the lives of children and protect people's health. One of the ways they are doing this is by making immunizations available to people who live in poor countries. There is always a lot of excitement when GAVI calls a press conference to announce a pledging event.

CHAPTER 2
Conquering Cancer

The process of conquering cancer involves education and prevention. It also requires research to find out more about what causes the disease and how it can be cured. The American Cancer Society is one of the most widely known philanthropies to focus on cancer and how it affects those who have it. The organization was founded in 1913 in New York City by a group of physicians and business leaders who first called it the American Society for the Control of Cancer. At the time the Society was founded, a diagnosis of cancer almost always ended with the death of the patient. The shame of having an incurable disease was so great that people often did not tell their friends and relatives that they had been diagnosed. Sometimes doctors did not even tell their own patients that they had cancer.

The founders of the American Society for the Control of Cancer knew they had to eliminate the stigma associated with cancer if progress were to be made in treating and curing the disease. They began educating people about the disease by writing articles about cancer and printing them in popular publications. In 1936, the Society began recruiting volunteers to raise money and further educate the public about cancer. In 1945, the American Society for the Control of Cancer was reorganized into the American Cancer Society. The next year, the American Cancer Society raised over $4 million, some of which went to establish their trailblazing research program. One of the first breakthroughs to come from research funded by the American Cancer Society was the discovery that childhood leukemia could be treated with the drug aminopterin. This research was conducted

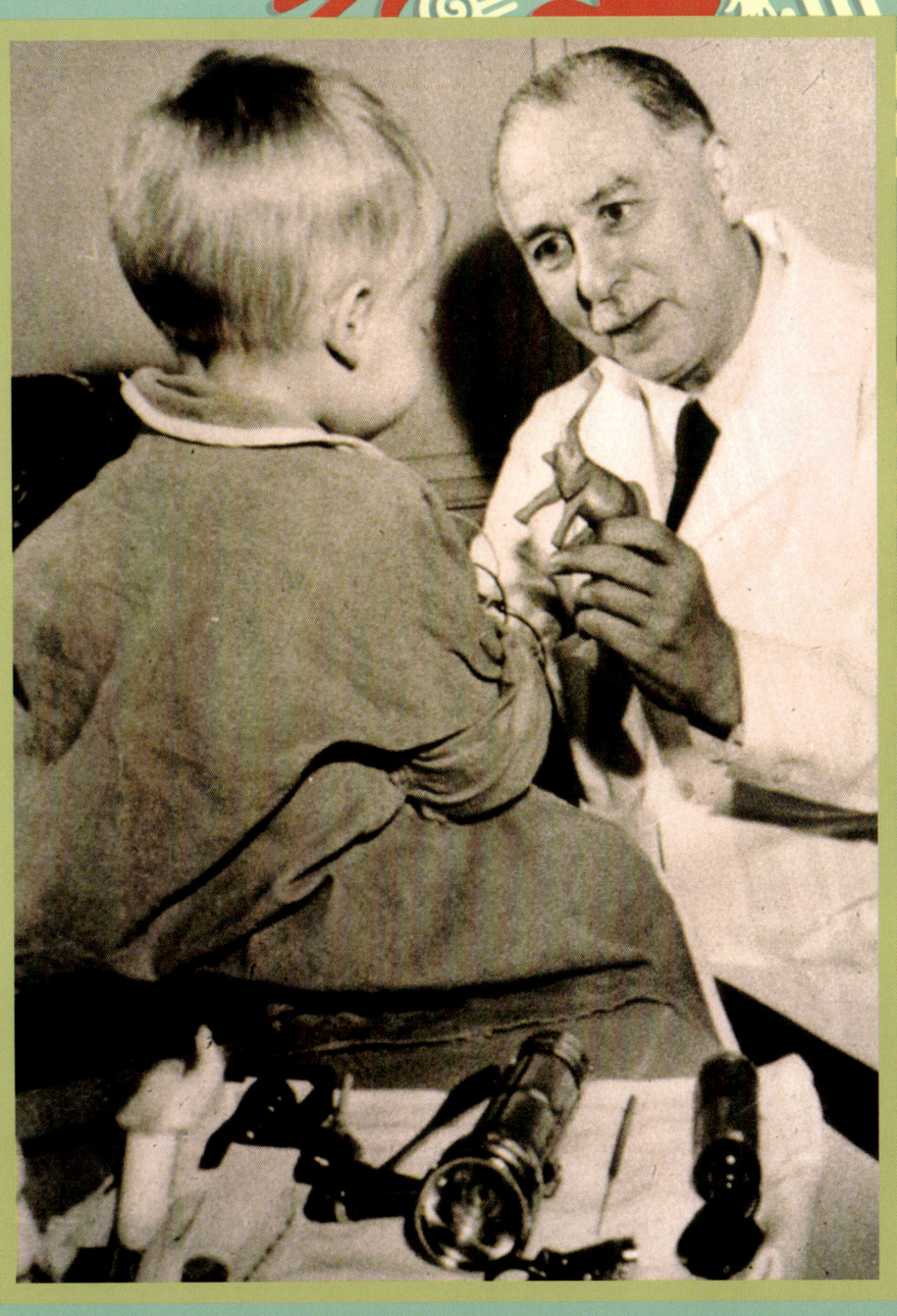

Working with the American Cancer Society, Dr. Sidney Farber showed that childhood leukemia could be put into remission with pharmaceutical drugs. In 1947, he founded the Children's Cancer Research Foundation. Today, the Dana-Farber Cancer Institute, located in Boston, bears his name.

Luminaria bags line a track where an American Cancer Society Relay for Life is being held. Relay for Life is a fundraiser held by the American Cancer Society. Relay participants can purchase these candle-lit bags and decorate them in honor of those who are battling or have battled cancer.

CONQUERING CANCER

at Harvard Medical School by Dr. Sidney Farber in 1947. His work with aminopterin led to the creation of other drugs that could also be used as chemotherapy agents to treat cancer. Dr. Farber's research earned him the title, "Father of Chemotherapy."[1]

Many of the major cancer breakthroughs since that time have been due, in part, to the American Cancer Society.[2] Since 1913, the organization has invested approximately $3.6 billion into research.[3] Some of the more well-known contributions of the American Cancer Society include the discovery of the link between cancer and smoking, and the development of screening tests to detect cancer early, before it has spread to other parts of the body. The American Cancer Society has been involved in the development of other types of cancer treatments, such as interferon. The Society has also funded research to increase the cure rate for childhood leukemia and other cancers.

Today the American Cancer Society is the largest nongovernmental supporter of cancer research in the United States. The Society spends approximately $130 million each year investigating possible cures for cancer.[4] The American Cancer Society raises money for research with donations and fundraisers, like Relay for Life. This is an overnight community fundraising walk that is done in teams around a track. Relay for Life is a major benefit activity for the American Cancer Society and thousands of people, many of whom are cancer survivors, participate. Since 1985, Relay for Life has raised nearly $5 billion to fight cancer.[5]

Currently the American Cancer Society is conducting two cancer prevention studies to determine which lifestyle, behavioral, environmental, and genetic factors may cause, or prevent, cancer.[6] The mission of the American Cancer Society is eliminating cancer as a major health problem by educating people about ways to stay healthy, helping those who have cancer get well, and researching cures. The American Cancer Society believes that one of the best ways to conquer cancer is to find it early, when it is easiest to treat. Prevention is just as important as a cure. The

Chapter 2

Society states that more than half of all cancer deaths could be avoided if people lived a healthy lifestyle by eating right, not smoking, and seeing their doctors regularly to get recommended cancer screenings. With the help of the American Cancer Society, there are nearly fourteen million cancer survivors alive today in the United States alone. Every day, more than four hundred lives are saved that would have otherwise been lost to cancer.[7]

A Sister's Promise Leads to a Worldwide Movement

Breast cancer is a disease that mostly affects women. Nancy G. Brinker's sister, Suzy was just thirty-six years old when she lost her battle with the disease on August 4, 1980. At the time, people did not talk much about breast cancer; it wasn't even polite to mention the word "breast" in public. Before she died, Suzy made Nancy promise to make people aware of breast cancer and end the shame that women with this type of cancer often felt. Nancy, who was diagnosed with breast cancer three years after Suzy died, promised her sister she would do all that she could to find a cure and end breast cancer forever. Nancy's promise to her sister became a worldwide movement to end breast cancer called the Susan G. Komen Breast Cancer Foundation. In 2007 its name was changed to Susan G. Komen for the Cure. "From early on, we were clear in our own minds about our mission: increase [breast cancer] awareness, fund research, and improve access to care," Nancy writes.[8] Above all, Nancy wanted to prevent other women from going through what Suzy went through. Her goal was, and continues to be, to conquer breast cancer by preventing the disease from attacking healthy women, and curing those who already have it.

Nancy started her philanthropy with $200 she had saved from her grocery money. In its early days, the foundation attracted donors who gave large sums of money. But Nancy believed it could do more. In 1983, she founded the Susan G. Komen Race for the Cure, a 5K race created to increase awareness about breast cancer while raising funds through sponsorship. The first Race

CONQUERING CANCER

Nancy Brinker, right, made a promise to her sister, Susan G. Komen, that she would fight to end the shame associated with breast cancer. Her philanthropy became Susan G. Komen for the Cure. Since it was founded in 1983, Susan G. Komen for the Cure has raised billions of dollars for breast cancer awareness and research.

for the Cure was held that same year in Dallas, Texas. More than eight hundred runners took part. Now, over one hundred Races for the Cure are held throughout the world each year, and more than one million runners participate. The Susan G. Komen Race for the cure is now the largest registered 5K race series in the world.[9]

In its first year, Susan G. Komen for the Cure gave $30,000 to two researchers who were researching breast cancer at separate locations in Texas. Over the past thirty years, the philanthropy

Hundreds of people run in the Susan G. Komen Race for the Cure on Saturday, January 25, 2014, in downtown West Palm Beach, Florida.

has invested almost $2 billion in ground-breaking research, services, and advocacy.[10] Susan G. Komen for the Cure also trains volunteers to reach out to members of the community who have breast cancer or participate in educational events. The foundation is active in more than fifty countries and has millions of volunteers throughout the world.

Since 1990, the work of Susan G. Komen for the Cure has helped to decrease breast cancer deaths in the United States by 33 percent.[11] Much of this has been accomplished by teaching women how to detect breast cancer when it's in the early stages. Like cancer in general, the earlier it is caught, the more easily it can be treated and the more likely it is to be cured.

What is Cancer?

Cancer is a general term that refers to a group of more than one hundred diseases.[12] Cancer occurs when the DNA, or genetic material, of one normal cell mutates, or undergoes a change. While some cell mutations result in beneficial changes for an organism, the mutation that causes a normal cell to become a cancer cell is not one of them. Changes in the DNA cause the cell to multiply out of control, and each new cell formed also contains the mutated DNA. Cancer is the result of mutated cells that have spread throughout the body or invaded other organs and tissues.

In the United States, it is estimated that one-half of all men and one-third of all women will develop cancer sometime during their lifetimes.[13] Only heart disease causes more deaths than cancer in the US.[14]

Cancer is often caused by a combination of factors, but the exact cause of most cancers is still unclear. The risk of getting some types of cancer is linked to certain behaviors, like smoking and excessive exposure to the sun. Some cancers are hereditary, and others are caused by environmental factors, like contact with lead or asbestos. About 20 percent of cancers are due to infections, mostly viruses.[15] Cancer is a noncommunicable disease, which means you can't get cancer from someone who has it.

Smoking has been linked to lung cancer and other types of cancer. Campaigns to make people aware of the dangers of smoking are saving lives by reducing the number of people who smoke.

CHAPTER 3
Conquering Communicable Diseases

One reason disease is difficult to conquer is that diseases are acquired in different ways. A great many diseases are caused by microorganisms, forms of life that can only be seen with a microscope, like bacteria and viruses. Commonly, we call microorganisms "germs." Germs live in the air we breathe, the food we eat, and the water we drink. Germs also infect insects, animals, and humans. Diseases that are caused by a microorganism entering the body are called infectious diseases. Infectious diseases often spread easily from person to person. Therefore infectious diseases can also be communicable diseases.

The Deadly Mosquito Bite

Malaria is an example of a preventable infectious disease. It is caused by a microscopic parasite and is spread by mosquitos. The symptoms of malaria are similar to those of the flu. If it is left untreated, malaria can lead to seizures, anemia, kidney failure, and other medical emergencies. According to the World Health Organization, an estimated 219 million cases of malaria occurred worldwide in 2010. There were 660,000 deaths, with 91 percent occurring in Africa. Eighty-six percent of deaths were in children under five years old.[1] Malaria is one of the top three killers of children worldwide. Every thirty seconds, a child dies from malaria.[2]

   One organization that is working towards conquering malaria is the Peace Corps. Although it is a governmental agency, the Peace Corps relies on volunteers and donations to carry out its mission of promoting world peace and friendship. The Peace

Diseases are transmitted in various ways. Those that are transmitted by mosquito are called mosquito-borne illnesses. Malaria, yellow fever, dengue fever, and encephalitis are examples of diseases that are spread by mosquitoes. Some philanthropies are working to show people how they can prevent these diseases by avoiding mosquitos altogether.

Chapter 3

Corps was officially started in 1961 as a means of giving ordinary citizens a way to make a difference in the world. To date, over 210,000 people have volunteered with the Peace Corps in 139 countries.[3]

Peace Corps volunteers are currently working on a program called "Stomp Out Malaria in Africa." Since malaria is transmitted by the bite of a mosquito, one way to prevent the disease is to keep the mosquitos from biting people in the first place. One such preventive measure is the use of mosquito netting. Peace Corps volunteers distribute netting fabric and show the community how to treat it with insecticide, turning it into a barrier against mosquitos that can be used when sleeping. The Peace Corps is working with other programs, such as President Obama's Malaria Initiative, a program to reduce deaths by malaria in specific countries in Africa by 50 percent, and Malaria No More, a New-York-based initiative working to eradicate malaria in Africa. The approach taken by these organizations, and others, like the Bill & Melinda Gates Foundation, is multi-directional: testing, treatment, and prevention. Health workers test people for malaria with an easy and quick blood test. Those who have the disease are treated with a combination of anti-malarial drugs. And research to develop a vaccine continues.

No More Polio

Poliomyelitis, often referred to as polio, is a crippling and sometimes fatal infectious disease caused by a virus that invades the brain and spinal cord. Polio viruses spread through contact with oral secretions and feces. In some cases, polio can weaken the muscles of the people who get it, making it difficult to swallow or perform normal activities, like walking. It can also lead to permanent paralysis or death. There is no cure for polio, but there are safe and effective vaccines to prevent it. Polio has been virtually eliminated in the developed world where vaccinations are common, but it has never been eradicated in Afghanistan, Nigeria, and Pakistan. And polio is reemerging in

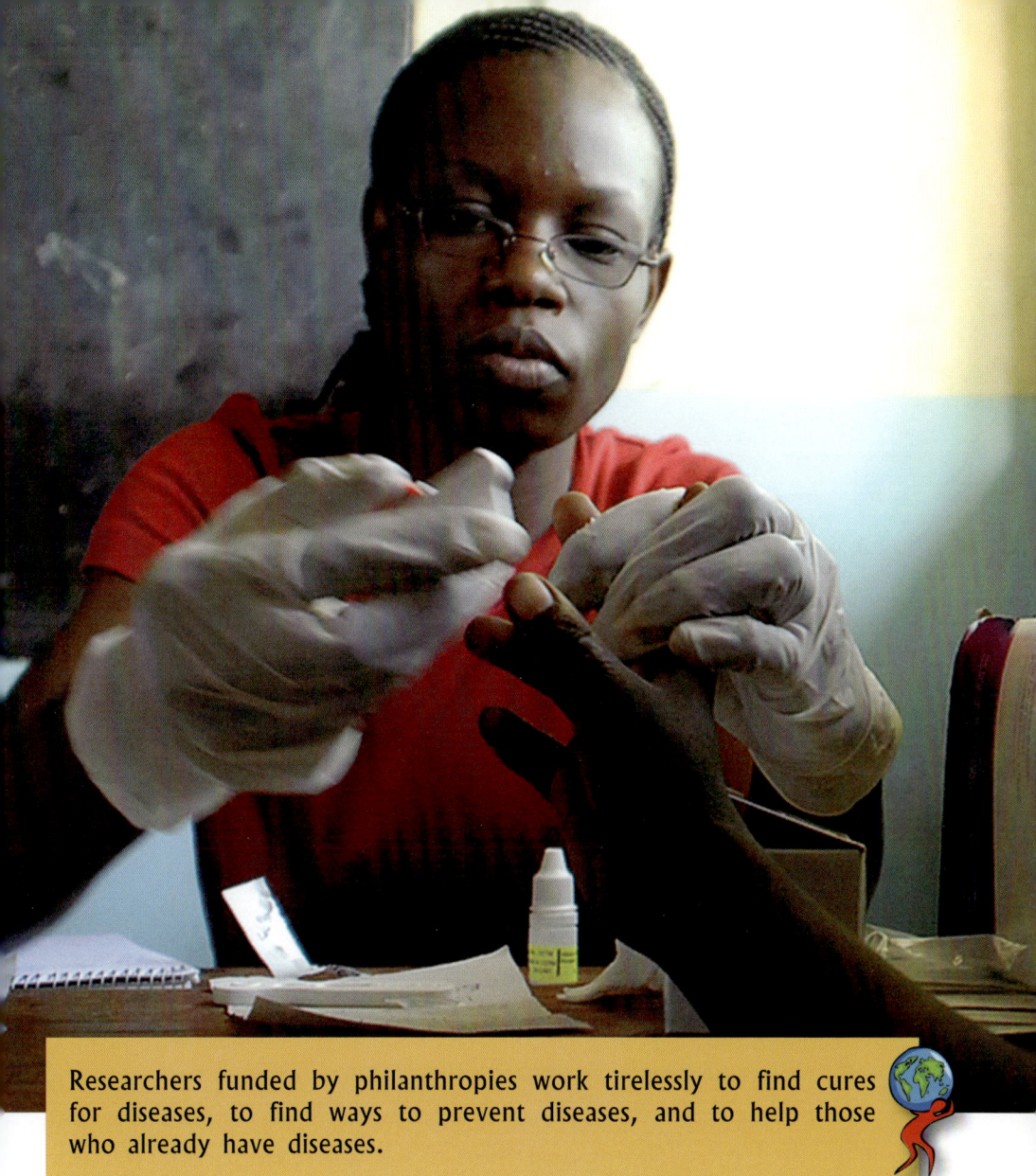

Researchers funded by philanthropies work tirelessly to find cures for diseases, to find ways to prevent diseases, and to help those who already have diseases.

some African countries, after having been previously eliminated. The best strategy to conquer polio is immunization with vaccines to stop transmission.[4]

One professional organization that is helping to conquer polio is Rotary International. This group was formed by Chicago attorney Paul P. Harris in 1905. The men called their group the Rotary Club because they planned to rotate their meeting place among their offices. As the number of Rotary Clubs increased,

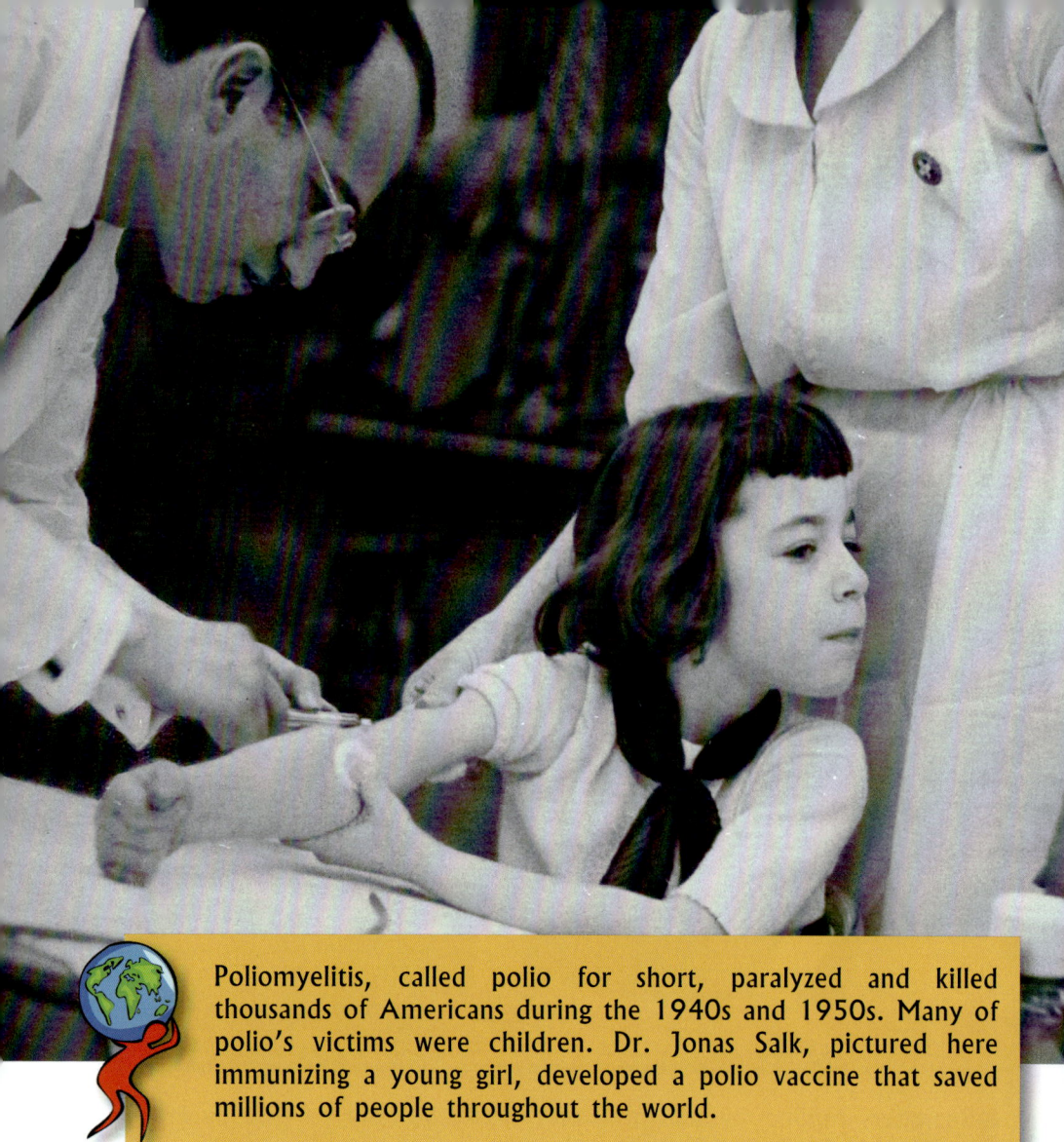

Poliomyelitis, called polio for short, paralyzed and killed thousands of Americans during the 1940s and 1950s. Many of polio's victims were children. Dr. Jonas Salk, pictured here immunizing a young girl, developed a polio vaccine that saved millions of people throughout the world.

first in the United States and then worldwide, the group became Rotary International.[5]

One of the missions of Rotary International is to do "good in the world."[6] An endowment was formed for this purpose in 1917, and in 1928, the philanthropy was named the Rotary Foundation. One of the first organizations that the Rotary Foundation helped was the National Society for Crippled Children. This group was started in 1919, and later changed its name to Easter Seals. Today, Easter Seals continues to help people with disabilities and special needs, and their families.

CONQUERING COMMUNICABLE DISEASES

The Rotary Foundation's commitment to end polio through vaccination began in 1979, when it helped purchase and deliver the polio vaccine to over six million children in the Philippines. In 1985, the Rotary Foundation started PolioPlus with an initial pledge of $120 million. At the time, more than 350,000 people throughout 125 countries were afflicted with polio each year. With this commitment, PolioPlus became the first and largest program that used private funds to support public health worldwide. Today other organizations, both philanthropic and governmental, are partnering with Rotary International to achieve worldwide elimination of polio by vaccination. UNICEF, the CDC, WHO, the Bill & Melinda Gates Foundation, governments around the world, and volunteers and donors contribute time and money to this cause.

The Rotary Foundation is also involved with the Global Polio Eradication Initiative. This partnership is led by the World Health Organization. Since 1988, the Rotary Foundation, and its partners in the Global Polio Eradication Initiative have immunized over 2.5 billion children. In that time, The number of polio cases has been reduced by 99 percent.[7]

"Willful Waste Makes Woeful Want"

John Davison Rockefeller's father was a shady character who was married to two women at the same time.[8] Despite his unstable upbringing, John managed to become founder of the Standard Oil Company, a position that made him the richest man in the world in his time. His mother's words, "willful waste makes woeful want," stayed with him all his life. Instead of wasting his fortune on things he did not need, he decided to use his money to make positive changes in the world. In 1901, he founded the Rockefeller Institute for Medical Research, which later became Rockefeller University.[9] In 1913, John established the Rockefeller Foundation to promote the well-being of humanity worldwide. "I believe it is my duty to go on making money and still more money, and to dispose of the money I make for the

Chapter 3

John D. Rockefeller (left) was part owner of a business before he was twenty years old. His business sense came naturally to him, but he also worked hard. He passed his work ethic on to his son, John D. Rockefeller, Jr. (right), who became a philanthropist in his own right.

good of my fellow man according to the dictates of my conscience," he once told a reporter who interviewed him.[10]

Today the Rockefeller Foundation works both within the United States and throughout the world. In addition to improving the health of people across the globe, the Rockefeller Foundation finds ways to encourage consumers and businesses to operate in ways that will not harm the environment, strengthen cities against natural and man-made disasters, and create jobs for people in developing countries. The Foundation's Disease Surveillance Networks (DSN) program was started in 2007 to focus on new infectious diseases with the potential to create a pandemic. DSN detects new diseases, monitors them, and gives information about them to nearby countries. The long-term goal of the DSN is to change the way governments and people in charge of a country's health care make decisions about new diseases.

Conquering AIDS

Acquired immunodeficiency syndrome (AIDS) was one of the most devastating new diseases to emerge in the twentieth century. Caused by the human immunodeficiency virus (HIV), AIDS is a condition in which the immune system is severely weakened. Without a healthy immune system, a number of diseases and problems can occur including loss of strength, pneumonia, and several types of cancers. AIDS was first reported by the CDC in 1981 after several young men began dying of mysterious illnesses.

The CDC estimates that today, in the United States, more than one million people are living with HIV. One in five, or 20 percent, of those who are HIV positive are unaware that they are infected.[11] Presently, there are 33.4 million people throughout the world living with HIV; 97 percent of these people live in low- and middle-income countries, particularly in sub-Saharan Africa.[12]

There is currently no cure or vaccine for AIDS. The International AIDS Society is the world's leading independent association of professionals working to fight HIV.[13] Based in Switzerland, the Society is active in the global fight against AIDS by organizing initiatives like the Towards an HIV Cure project. The project brings scientists from around the world together to work to find a cure for AIDS. Other philanthropic agencies that are helping conquer AIDS are AVERT, which is based in the United Kingdom, and the Elton John AIDS Foundation, which has its headquarters in New York City.

Performer Elton John founded the Elton John AIDS Foundation after young teenager Ryan White died from AIDS. White was infected by a blood transfusion before it was understood how the disease was transmitted.

CHAPTER 4
Big Steps Forward

Doctors Without Borders (also known as Médecins Sans Frontières) is an international organization made up of medical staff from dozens of countries. The organization, which was started in 1971, provides emergency medical help to people in over sixty countries.[1] Doctors Without Borders helps those affected by wars, epidemics, malnutrition, and natural disasters. It also helps people who are excluded from their country's healthcare system due to discrimination or neglect. The organization provides medical help without considering race, religion, or politics.[2] Doctors Without Borders believes that all victims of conflict and disaster deserve assistance and protection, and that need should be the only criteria used to judge whether or not Doctors Without Borders will help.[3]

In the past, Doctors Without Borders has responded to outbreaks of cholera, meningitis, measles, malaria, and other infectious diseases. All of these diseases are contagious and can spread rapidly within a community; some can kill hundreds of people within weeks.[4] Doctors Without Borders also treats people who have HIV/AIDS and tuberculosis. In addition, medical staff treat those who have kala azar, a disease caused by a parasite that leads to swelling of the liver and spleen; sleeping sickness, a disease spread by the tsetse fly that can affect the central nervous system; and Chagas disease, an illness spread by insects that causes problems in the heart and digestive system. These three diseases are relatively unknown in developed countries, like the United States, but they appear in poor countries where health

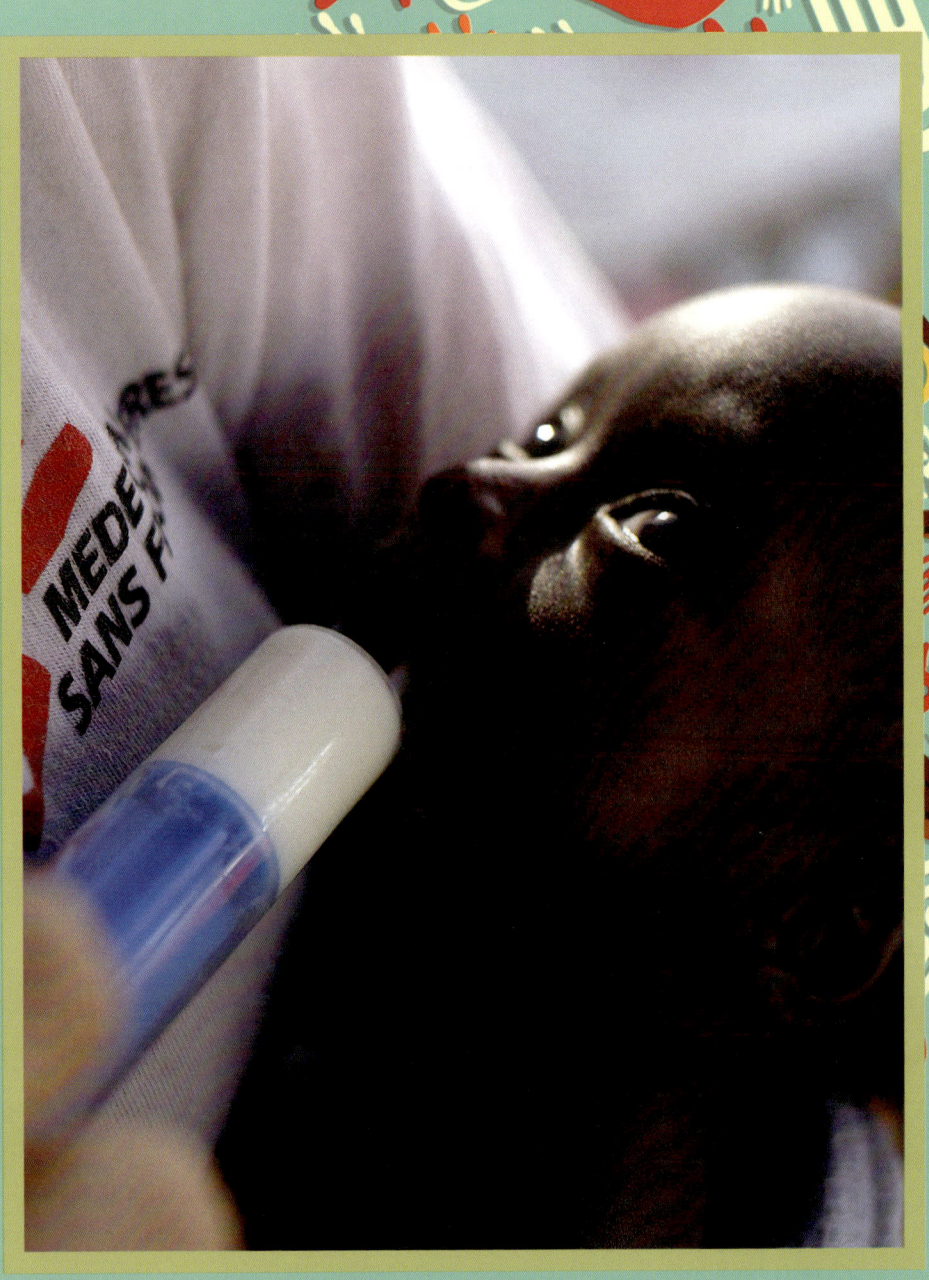

In Juba, South Sudan, a malnourished six-week-old orphan is cradled by a nurse working for Doctors Without Borders (Médecins Sans Frontières). The emergency charity does not take sides or participate in political situations; its mission is to help people in need.

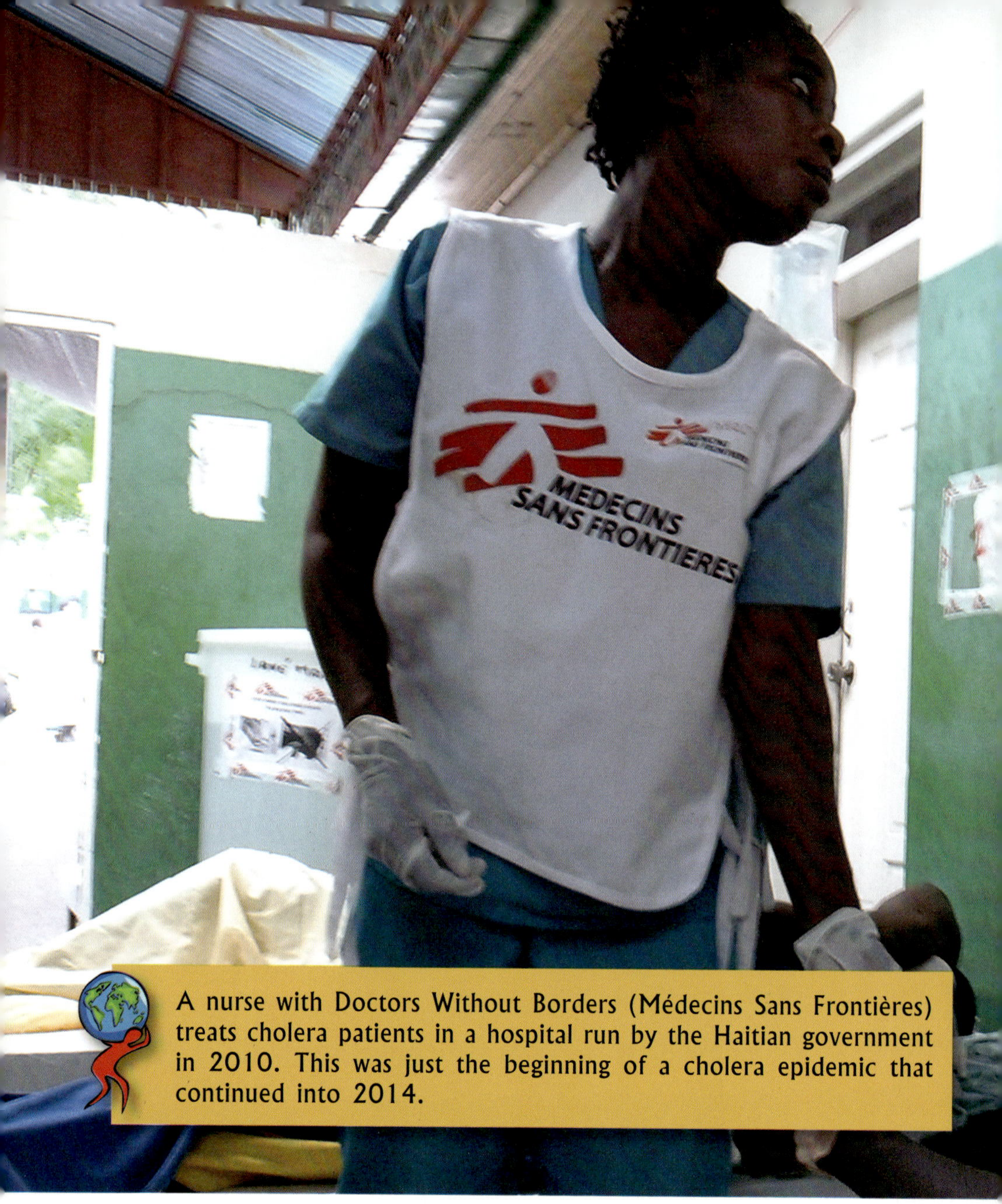

A nurse with Doctors Without Borders (Médecins Sans Frontières) treats cholera patients in a hospital run by the Haitian government in 2010. This was just the beginning of a cholera epidemic that continued into 2014.

care is limited. For this reason, kala azar, sleeping sickness, and Chagas disease are sometimes referred to as "neglected diseases."[5]

In 1999, Doctors Without Borders began its Access Campaign. This initiative pushes for the availability and development of new medications that save and prolong the lives of those with serious illnesses. The program also encourages the development of diagnostic tests and vaccines. Doctors Without Borders is

especially interested in the progress of medicines, diagnostic tests, and cures of the diseases that affect children most.

Although it remains politically neutral, Doctors Without Borders supports governments in their efforts to improve health care. In 2010, the organization worked with the governments of the African countries of Niger and Mali to deliver vaccines to over one million children and young adults. These vaccines

Chapter 4

protect against meningitis, a serious and often deadly infection of the protective area that surrounds the brain and spinal cord.

Conquering Obesity

Dr. Robert Atkins was a cardiologist who believed that a healthy diet and good nutrition were the keys to good health. He was especially concerned about heart disease, diabetes, and obesity, which are three medical conditions that can be prevented and controlled by diet. Dr. Atkins designed a weight loss program which restricted carbohydrates in the diet, but allowed fats and proteins. His book about his diet, *Dr. Atkins' New Diet Revolution* became a popular bestseller. In 1999, Dr. Atkins and his wife Veronica established a private foundation. Its purpose was to provide funding for scientific research into the obesity epidemic. He wanted scientists to study nutrition and metabolism and how they contribute to obesity.

When Dr. Atkins died in 2003, his wife Veronica became chair of the foundation and continued his work. Today, the Dr. Robert C. and Veronica Atkins Foundation has expanded to include the study of the relationship between nutrition and other health conditions, including cancer and Alzheimer's disease. In addition, the Atkins Foundation aims to eradicate childhood obesity and type 2 diabetes, a disease that causes too much glucose, or sugar, to be present in the blood.[6]

Conquering Asthma

Herb and Marion Sandler are former bankers who owned Golden West Financial Corporation. In 2006, the Sandlers made over $25 billion when they sold their company. They put $1.3 billion into the Sandler Foundation, a small foundation they had been using to fund worthwhile projects. One of the causes the Sandlers support is the study of asthma. Since 2000, the Sandler Foundation has donated more than $100 million to the research of this disease.[7] This chronic disease of the lungs affects twenty-five million Americans. Each year almost 3,500 Americans die from

Dr. Robert Atkins spent his life teaching people that there is a connection between nutrition and good health. After his death, his philanthropy, the Atkins Foundation, continued to provide millions of dollars for nutrition research.

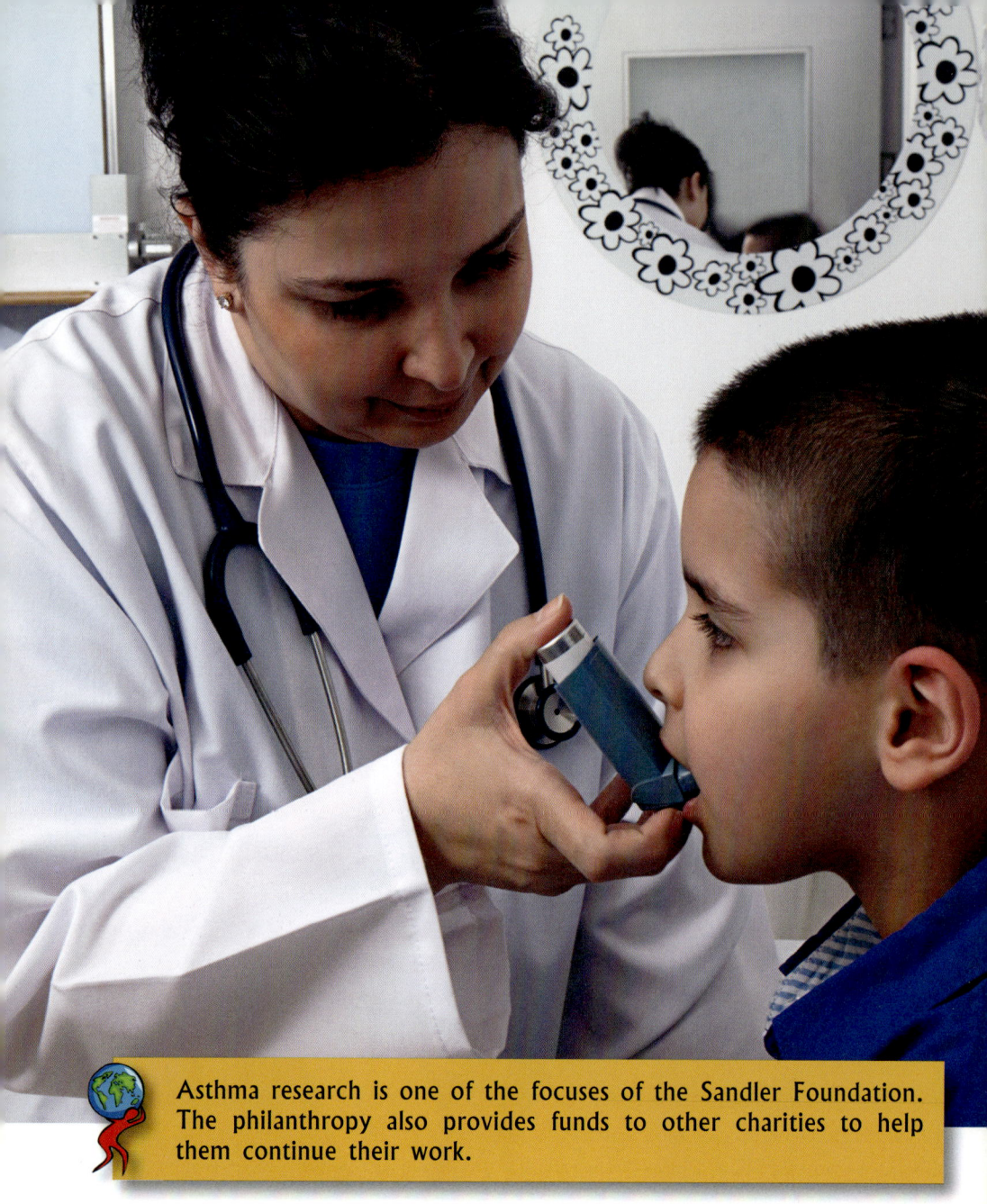

Asthma research is one of the focuses of the Sandler Foundation. The philanthropy also provides funds to other charities to help them continue their work.

asthma.[8] The Sandler Foundation has sponsored research that has led to advances in asthma medications. Five new medications are now being tested in clinical trials.[9]

Conquering Smallpox

Smallpox was a viral disease that only affected humans. The disease caused pus-filled blisters to form on the body. The virus was spread through contact with the pus in the blisters. The disease existed for at least three thousand years, as Egyptian mummies show evidence of the disease.[10] Throughout history, many smallpox epidemics occurred in which millions of people died. Most of those who did not lose their lives to the disease were left scarred and sometimes blind. After they recovered, however, they developed an immunity that protected them from reinfection by the smallpox virus for the rest of their lives.

In 1950, under the direction of the Pan American Health Organization, smallpox was eradicated in all American countries except Argentina, Brazil, Colombia, and Ecuador. Still, millions of people continued to die of smallpox in Africa, India, and elsewhere. In 1967, the World Health Organization organized an effort to globally eliminate smallpox. This was accomplished through containment and "ring vaccination." Anyone showing the signs or symptoms of smallpox was contained, so as not to spread the disease to others. Anyone who was close to someone with smallpox was considered to have been exposed to the virus; these people were vaccinated. The last case of naturally occurring smallpox occurred in Somalia in 1977. Three years later, the World Health Assembly announced that smallpox had been eradicated.[11]

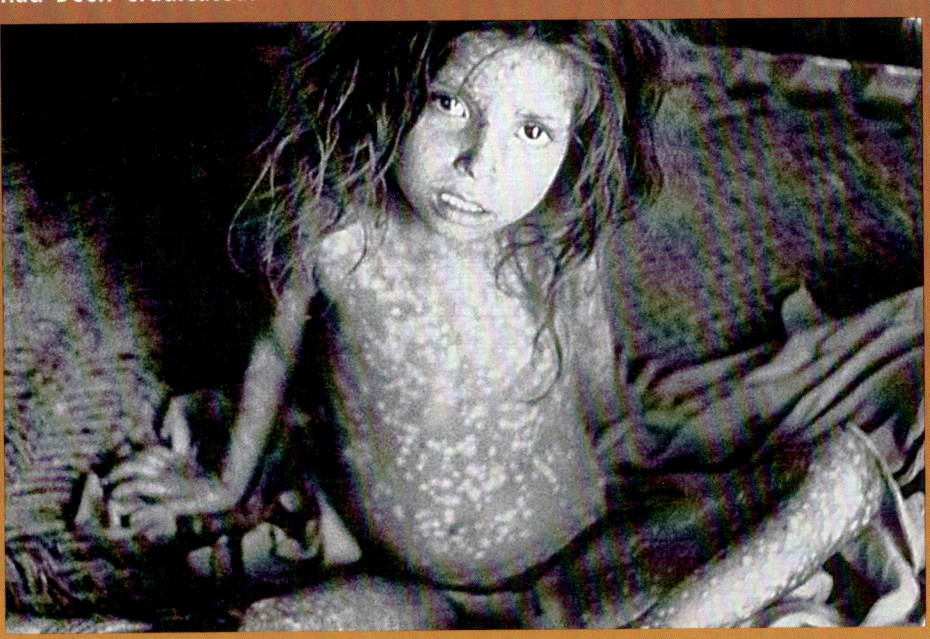

Child with smallpox.

CHAPTER 5

You Can Help, Too!

People all over the world are working towards the day when disease is conquered. Clearly, philanthropies are playing an important role in achieving this goal. What would a disease-free world look like? It would be a place where cures for all diseases are readily available to all, and those who are afflicted with a disease would receive the medicines needed to become well. Preventable diseases would no longer affect people because everyone would have access to vaccines and other means of stopping diseases before they spread. Clean water and safe food, two important allies in the fight against disease, would also be available to everyone. So would adequate housing and working conditions, and acceptable standards of sanitation and hygiene. Living and work spaces would be free from harmful substances which cause disease, like asbestos and lead. People would make wise lifestyle choices and avoid behaviors, like smoking, that have the potential to make them sick.

You can help conquer disease too! The philanthropies mentioned in this book are just a sampling of the many worthwhile organizations that are tirelessly working to achieve this goal.

All of them depend on donations to keep their work going. If you would like to contribute money to a philanthropy, check it out first. Websites like Charity Navigator (www.charitynavigator.org), or Great Nonprofits (www.greatnonprofits.org) are good places to see if a philanthropy can be counted on to do what it claims to do.

Giving money is not the only way to help conquer disease. There are lots of other ways to help. Start in your own community

UNICEF Goodwill Ambassador David Beckham helps children affected by Typhoon Haiyan paint a wall mural at a UNICEF-supported school. The typhoon destroyed parts of the Philippines in November 2013. Acute respiratory infections, fever, diarrhea, hypertension, skin diseases, and wound infections increased as a result of the typhoon.

Chapter 5

Alexandra Scott was diagnosed with cancer when she was just one year old. When she was four, she asked her parents if she could start a lemonade stand and give the money she made to doctors so they could help other sick kids. The idea spread throughout the world, and when she died at age eight, her parents Jay (far left) and Liz (far right) continued Alex's Lemonade Stand. Here, popular Los Angeles chefs (center, left to right) David Lentz, Caroline Styne, and Suzanne Goin are on hand to prepare special dishes for guests of the 2013 fundraising event LA Loves Alex's Lemonade.

to look for ways that you can volunteer a few hours a week. Many philanthropies have local offices where you can staff telephones, perform clerical duties, and even learn to train other volunteers. Perhaps you can participate in a local fundraiser, like a walk-a-thon or 5K race where the proceeds go to a medical philanthropy. "What You Can Do to Help" in the back of this book lists other ways that you can help.

Whether you contribute money or time, you should feel good knowing that you are doing your part to make the world disease-free. If we all do what we can, disease will be conquered. It's just a matter of time.

Conquering Disease

There are many more diseases that need to be conquered than are described in this book. Microorganisms like bacteria, viruses, and parasites are not the only causes of disease. Some diseases, like the blood disorder sickle cell anemia, are inherited conditions passed through genes from parent to child. Others, such as the lung disease asbestosis, are caused by harmful things in the environment. Still others, called autoimmune diseases, occur when the body's immune system attacks a part of the body the way it would attack a virus or bacterium. Rheumatoid arthritis is an example of an autoimmune disease. Stress causes disease. So does a lack of good nutrition and clean drinking water.

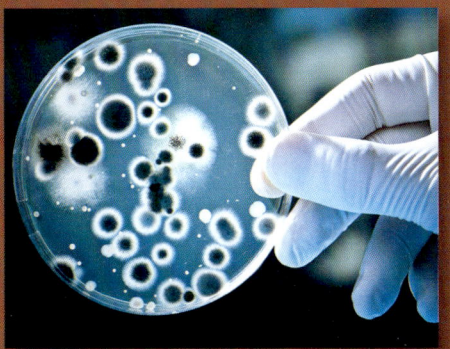

In order to study bacteria, scientists grow them in petri dishes. The dishes are filled with a gelatin containing nutrients that encourage bacterial growth.

Even though we are making headway against disease, we cannot let down our guard. New diseases continue to emerge even as cures and ways to prevent existing diseases are found. Many new diseases still have no treatments, cures, or vaccines. In addition, some diseases are spreading to new geographical areas. And some diseases are becoming resistant to the medications used to treat them. Countries like the United States face different challenges when it comes to eliminating disease. A free society allows people to take charge of their own lives, including their health. Unfortunately, some people choose to overeat, smoke tobacco, abuse alcohol, use street drugs, and behave in other ways that put good health at risk. Therefore, education has an important role in conquering disease.

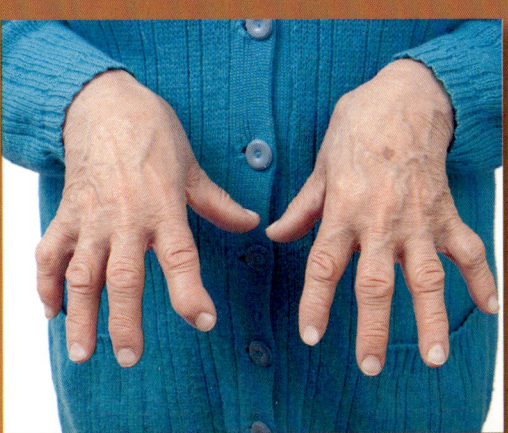

Rheumatoid arthritis is an autoimmune disease that causes swollen and painful joints.

WHAT YOU CAN DO TO HELP

Hold a lemonade sale in your front yard. Donate your profits to help children with cancer. Find out how at the Alex's Lemonade Stand Foundation website: http://www.alexslemonade.org/campaign/kids-corner/how-have-lemonade-stand

The SickKids Foundation has fundraising ideas for kids on its website: http://www.sickkidsfoundation.com/kidsbelieve/

Send "happy mail" to a sick child. http://www.hugsandhope.org/kidslist.htm

Contact your local hospital or medical center to learn about volunteer opportunities.

CHAPTER NOTES

Chapter 1: Conquering Childhood Diseases

1. Samuel H. Preston and Michael R. Haines, *Fatal Years: Child Mortality in Late Nineteenth-Century America* (Princeton, NJ: Princeton University Press, 1991), pp. 3–5.
2. CDC, *MMWR*, "Achievements in Public Health, 1900–1999: Healthier Mothers and Babies," October 1, 1999.
3. American Red Cross, "Tsunami Recovery Program: Five Year Report," 2009, p. 3.
4. American Red Cross, "Bringing Help, Bringing Hope: The American Red Cross Response to Hurricanes Katrina, Rita and Wilma," 2010.
5. Deafness Foundation, "Rubella," April 2009.
6. Measles & Rubella Initiative, "The Commitments."
7. Measles & Rubella Initiative, "Mid-Year 2013: Measles and Rubella So Far," July 9, 2013.
8. Ibid.
9. Bill & Melinda Gates Foundation. http://www.gatesfoundation.org
10. The GAVI Alliance, "Progress Report 2012," p. 7.
11. Ibid., p. 4.

Chapter 2: Conquering Cancer

1. American Cancer Society, "Our History," June 13, 2013.
2. Ibid.
3. Ibid.
4. American Cancer Society, "Your DetermiNation Cancer Fundraising Dollars at Work."
5. American Cancer Society, Relay for Life, "What Is Relay?"
6. American Cancer Society, "Current Cancer Prevention Studies."
7. American Cancer Society, "Our History," June 13, 2013.
8. Nancy G. Brinker, *Promise Me: How a Sister's Love Launched the Global Movement to End Breast Cancer* (New York: Crown Publishing Group, 2010), p. 209.
9. Susan G. Komen Race for the Cure, "About the Race."
10. Susan G. Komen, "Our Work," 2013.
11. Ibid.
12. American Cancer Society, "What Is Cancer?" March 21, 2012.
13. Ibid.
14. American Cancer Society, "Cancer Facts & Figures 2013."
15. William H. Chambers, *Expert Voices*, "Cancer Vaccines—Fulfilling the Promise," American Cancer Society, June 26, 2012.

Chapter 3: Conquering Communicable Diseases

1. CDC, Global Health—Division of Parasitic Diseases and Malaria, "Malaria Facts," September 19, 2012.
2. Malaria Foundation International, "What Is Malaria?" 2013.
3. Peace Corps, "Fast Facts," June 12, 2013.
4. CDC, Global Health, "What Is Polio?" September 3, 2013.
5. Rotary International, "History," 2013.
6. Rotary International, "Doing Good in the World," 2013.
7. Global Polio Eradication Initiative, "History," 2010.
8. Ron Chernow, *Titan: The Life of John D. Rockefeller, Sr.* (New York: Random House, 1998), p. 43.
9. Jeffrey David Brison, *Rockefeller, Carnegie, & Canada: American Philanthropy and the Arts & Letters in Canada* (Montreal: McGill-Queen's University Press, 2005), p. 27.
10. Grant Segall, *John D. Rockefeller: Anointed with Oil* (New York: Oxford University Press, 2001), p. 7.
11. AIDS.gov, "U.S. Statistics," June 6, 2012.
12. AIDS.gov, "Global AIDS Overview," June 1, 2012.
13. International AIDS Society, "About the IAS," 2013.

Chapter 4: Big Steps Forward

1. Doctors Without Borders, "History & Principles," 2013.
2. Doctors Without Borders, "How We Work," 2013.
3. James Orbinski, *An Imperfect Offering* (New York: Walker Publishing Company, 2008), p. 69.
4. Ibid., p. 144.
5. Doctors Without Borders, "How We Work," 2013.
6. The Dr. Robert C. and Veronica Atkins Foundation. http://www.atkinsfoundation.org/
7. Sandler Foundation, "Philanthropy," 2013.
8. American Asthma Foundation, "The Impact of Asthma," 2013.
9. Sandler Foundation, "Philanthropy," 2013.
10. National Geographic, "Smallpox: Conquered Killer."
11. The College of Physicians of Philadelphia, "Disease Eradication," The History of Vaccines.

Full citations, including web addresses, can be found in Works Consulted.

FURTHER READING

Books

Farrell, Jeanette. *Invisible Enemies: Stories of Infectious Disease.* New York: Farrar, Straus and Giroux, 2005.

Friedlander, Mark P. Jr. *Outbreak: Disease Detectives at Work.* Minneapolis, MN: Twenty-First Century Books: 2009.

Laughlin, Rosemary. *John D. Rockefeller: Oil Baron and Philanthropist.* Greensboro, NC: Morgan Reynolds, 2004.

Parry, Ann. *Doctors Without Borders: Médecins Sans Frontières.* Philadelphia: Chelsea House Publishers, 2005.

Sherrow, Victoria. *Polio Epidemic: Crippling Virus Outbreak.* Berkeley Heights, NJ: Enslow Publishers, 2001.

Somervill, Barbara. *Clara Barton: Founder of the American Red Cross.* Minneapolis, MN: Compass Point Books, 2007.

Ward, Brian. *Epidemic.* New York: Dorling Kindersley, 2000.

On the Internet

Centers for Disease Control and Prevention
http://www.cdc.gov/

Charity Navigator
http://charitynavigator.org/

Great Nonprofits
http://greatnonprofits.org/

The History of Vaccines
http://www.historyofvaccines.org/

Measles & Rubella Initiative
http://www.measlesrubellainitiative.org/

Peace Corps
http://www.peacecorps.gov/

Susan G. Komen for the Cure
http://ww5.komen.org/

Works Consulted

AIDS.gov. "Global AIDS Overview." June 1, 2012. http://aids.gov/federal-resources/around-the-world/global-aids-overview/index.html

AIDS.gov. "U.S. Statistics." June 6, 2012. http://aids.gov/hiv-aids-basics/hiv-aids-101/statistics/

American Asthma Foundation. "The Impact of Asthma." 2013. http://www.americanasthmafoundation.org/impact-asthma

American Cancer Society. "Cancer Facts & Figures 2013." http://www.cancer.org/research/cancerfactsstatistics/cancerfactsfigures2013/index

American Cancer Society. "Current Cancer Prevention Studies." http://www.cancer.org/research/researchtopreventcancer/currentcancerpreventionstudies/index

American Cancer Society. "Our History." June 13, 2013. http://www.cancer.org/aboutus/whoweare/our-history

American Cancer Society. Relay for Life. "What Is Relay?" http://www.relayforlife.org/learn/whatisrelay/index

American Cancer Society. "What Is Cancer?" March 21, 2012. http://www.cancer.org/cancer/cancerbasics/what-is-cancer

American Cancer Society. "Your DetermiNation Cancer Fundraising Dollars at Work." http://www.cancer.org/involved/participate/determination/your-determination-dollars-at-work

American Red Cross. "Tsunami Recovery Program: Five Year Report." 2009. http://www.redcross.org/images/MEDIA_CustomProductCatalog/m3140120_TsunamiRP5yearReport.pdf

Bill & Melinda Gates Foundation. http://www.gatesfoundation.org/

Brinker, Nancy G. *Promise Me: How a Sister's Love Launched the Global Movement to End Breast Cancer.* New York: Crown Publishing Group, 2010.

CDC. "Achievements in Public Health, 1900-1999: Healthier Mothers and Babies." *MMWR,* October 1, 1999. http://www.cdc.gov/mmwr/preview/mmwrhtml/mm4838a2.htm

CDC, Global Health—Division of Parasitic Diseases and Malaria. "Malaria Facts." September 19, 2012. http://www.cdc.gov/malaria/about/facts.html

CDC, Global Health, "What Is Polio?" September 3, 2013. http://www.cdc.gov/polio/about/

Chernow, Ron. *Titan: The Life of John D. Rockefeller, Sr.* New York: Random House, 1998.

The College of Physicians of Philadelphia. "Disease Eradication." The History of Vaccines. http://www.historyofvaccines.org/content/articles/disease-eradication

Delaet, Debra L., and David E. Delaet. *Global Health in the 21st Century: The Globalization of Disease and Wellness.* Boulder, CO: Paradigm Publishers, 2012.

Doctors Without Borders. "History & Principles." 2013. http://www.doctorswithoutborders.org/aboutus/?id=5226&cat=about-us-pages

The Dr. Robert C. and Veronica Atkins Foundation. http://www.atkinsfoundation.org/

End Polio Now. http://www.endpolio.org/

Forward, David C. *A Century of Service: The Story of Rotary International.* Evanston, IL: Rotary International, 2003.

The GAVI Alliance. "Progress Report 2012." http://www.gavialliance.org/library/publications/gavi-progress-reports/gavi-alliance-progress-report-2012/

FURTHER READING

Global Polio Eradication Initiative. "History." 2010. http://www.polioeradication.org/Aboutus/History.aspx

The History of Vaccines. http://www.historyofvaccines.org/

International AIDS Society. "About the IAS." 2013. http://www.iasociety.org/Default.aspx?pageId=2

Malaria Foundation International. "What Is Malaria?" 2013. http://www.malaria.org/index.php?option=com_content&task=section&id=8&Itemid=32

Maskalyk, James. *Six Months in Sudan: A Young Doctor in a War-Torn Village.* New York: Spiegel & Grau, 2009.

Measles & Rubella Initiative. http://www.measlesrubellainitiative.org/

Measles & Rubella Initiative. "Mid-Year 2013: Measles and Rubella So Far." July 9, 2013. http://www.measlesrubellainitiative.org/measles-outbreaks-mid-year-2013-update/

Nocera, Joe. "Self-Made Philanthropists." *The New York Times.* March 9, 2008.

Peace Corps. "Fast Facts." June 12, 2013. http://www.peacecorps.gov/about/fastfacts

Preston, Samuel H., and Michael R. Haines. *Fatal Years: Child Mortality in Late Nineteenth-Century America.* Princeton, NJ: Princeton University Press, 1991. http://www.nber.org/chapters/c11541.pdf

Rogak, Lisa. *Dr. Robert Atkins: The True Story of the Man Behind the War on Carbohydrates.* New York: Chamberlain Bros., 2005.

Rotary International. "History." 2013. https://www.rotary.org/en/history

Rotary International. "History of the Rotary Foundation." 2013. https://www.rotary.org/myrotary/en/rotary-foundation/history-rotary-foundation

Sandler Foundation. "Philanthropy." 2013. http://www.herbsandler.com/philanthropy/

Segall, Grant. *John D. Rockefeller: Anointed with Oil.* New York: Oxford University Press, 2001.

Susan G. Komen. "Our Work." 2013. http://ww5.komen.org/AboutUs/OurWork.html

Susan G. Komen Race for the Cure. "About the Race." http://apps.komen.org/raceforthecure/

Wolff, Jonathan. *The Human Right to Health.* New York: W.W. Norton & Co., 2012.

Youngerman, Barry. *Pandemics and Global Health.* New York: Infobase Publishing, 2008.

Yun, Oliver. "A New Meningitis Vaccine Brings Hope." Doctors Without Borders, January 31, 2011. http://www.doctorswithoutborders.org/publications/alert/article.cfm?id=5008&cat=alert-article

PHOTO CREDITS: All design elements from Photos.com/Sharon Beck; Cover, p. 1—Photos.com; pp. 4, 41 (bottom)—Thinkstock; pp. 7, 28—Library of Congress; pp. 8-9—FEMA; p. 11—Catherine Yeulet/Photos.com; p. 12—Jon Hrusa GDA Photo Service/Newscom; p.13—DFID - UK Department for International Development; p.15—National Institutes of Health; p. 16—U.S. Navy photo by Mass Communication Specialist 2nd Class Tucker M. Yates; p. 19 Norbert Vitéz/US Department of State; p. 20—Thomas Cordy/ZUMA Press/Newscom; p. 21—Jupiter Images/Photos.com; p. 23—Henrik Larsson/Photos.com; p.25—US Army Africa; p. 26—AKG Images/Newscom; p. 29—Paul Hennessy/Polaris/Newscom; p. 31—Hannah Mcneish/AFP/Getty Images/Newscom; pp. 32-33—Spencer Platt/Thinkstock; p. 35—John Barrett/ZUMAPRESS/Newscom; p. 36—Levent Konuk/Thinkstock; p. 37—CDC/US Department of Health and Human Services; p. 39—WENN Photos/Newscom; p. 40—Alex J. Berliner/AP Images; p. 41 (top)—Alexander Raths/Thinkstock

GLOSSARY

anemia (uh-NEE-mee-uh)—A blood disorder which can cause weakness and shortness of breath.

antitoxin (an-ti-TOK-sin)—A substance made by the body that fights against a specific toxin.

bacterium (bak-TEER-ee-uhm)—A microscopic life form; certain types of bacteria can cause disease in humans.

carbohydrate (kahr-boh-HAHY-dreyt)—A compound (such as a sugar) that exists in food, which supplies energy to the animals that eat it.

cardiologist (kahr-dee-OL-uh-jist)—A doctor who specializes in the health of the heart.

central nervous system (SEN-truhl NUR-vuhs SIS-tuhm)—The system of nerves in the brain and spine.

chemotherapy (kee-moh-THER-uh-pee)—Cancer treatment by chemical drugs which can destroy cancer cells.

chronic (KRON-ik)—Lasting a long time.

clinical trial (KLIN-i-kuhl TRAHY-uhl)—A test of a new drug or treatment to study its effectiveness and safety.

communicable (kuh-MYOO-ni-kuh-buhl)—Able to be passed from one person to another.

GLOSSARY

congenital (kuhn-JEN-i-tl) — Related to a condition that exists from birth.
contaminated (kuhn-TAM-uh-neyt-id) — Unclean or impure and harmful.
contract (kuhn-TRAKT) — To get or acquire by exposure.
criteria (krahy-TEER-ee-uh) — A standard or way of judging something.
diagnose (DAHY-uhg-nohs) — To identify a disease or illness.
diet (DAHY-it) — The food and drink eaten by a person.
digestive system (dih-JES-tiv SIS-tuhm) — The system of the body which takes in food, absorbs nutrients, and removes waste.
drug — A chemical that is used to treat, cure, or prevent a disease.
epidemic (ep-i-DEM-ik) — Affecting many people at the same time, and spreading from one person to another.
endowment (en-DOU-muhnt) — A fund or source of income.
eradicate (ih-RAD-i-cate) — To do away with, to eliminate from the world.
fat — Greasy substance that is part of plants and animals.
fatal (FEYT-ul) — Causing death or able to cause death.
feces (FEE-sees) — The waste that is released from the body after food is digested.
grassroots (GRAS-roots) — Activity done by ordinary people.
hereditary (huh-RED-i-ter-ee) — Capable of being passed from parent to child through genes.
humanitarian (hyoo-man-i-TAIR-ee-uhn) — Having concern for the well-being of people.
hygiene (HAHY-jeen) — A practice which helps people to stay healthy, such as cleanliness.
immune (ih-MYOON) — Protected from a disease.
industrialized (in-DUHS-tree-uh-lahyzd) — Relying on new technologies and industries more than older businesses such as farming and craftsmanship.
infection (in-FEK-shuhn) — The state of being affected by or contaminated with germs that cause disease.
infectious (in-FEK-shuhs) — Spread by infection.
initiative (ih-NISH-ee-uh-tiv) — An action that gets a movement started.
interferon (in-ter-FEER-on) — A protein that is made by the human body to inhibit a virus, bacteria, parasite, or tumor cell. Man-made versions of interferon can be used to treat diseases like cancer.
kidney (KID-nee) — One of a pair of organs located near the lower back that process waste fluids in the body.
liver (LIV-er) — An organ located in the abdominal/pelvic area that removes toxins from the body and creates proteins.
magnitude (MAG-ni-tood) — A measure of the size of an earthquake.
metabolism (muh-TAB-uh-liz-uhm) — The processes by which the body maintains itself by taking in and using energy.
microorganism (mahy-kroh-AWR-guh-niz-uhm) — A life form that is too small to be seen by the naked eye.
microscopic (mahy-kruh-SKOP-ik) — Something that is too small to be seen without a microscope.
neutral (NOO-truhl) — Not supporting any side in a disagreement.
nutrition (noo-TRISH-uhn) — The science or study of how the body uses food.
oral (AWR-uhl) — Related to the mouth.
pandemic (pan-DEM-ik) — An epidemic that has spread over a large area or the world.
paralysis (puh-RAL-uh-sis) — Loss of the ability to move a body part.
parasite (PAR-uh-sahyt) — An organism that lives in or on another organism of a different species.
politics (POL-i-tiks) — The affairs of a government.
protein (PROH-teen) — A substance that is used to build and maintain much of the body.
sanitation (san-i-TEY-shuhn) — The disposal of sewage and waste.
secretion (si-KREE-shuhn) — The act of releasing a substance from a cell.
seizure (SEE-zher) — A sudden attack that may cause the body to move violently.
spinal cord (SPAHYN-l KAWRD) — The cord of nerve tissue that runs from the brain down the back, which sends signals from the brain to the rest of the body.
spleen — The organ located below the left lung which filters blood, and contains cells that are part of the immune response.
sponsor (SPON-ser) — To pledge or promise money to another, often for a specific purpose.
stigma (STIG-muh) — A mark against or a bad feeling about something.
succumb (suh-KUHM) — To give in to or to die from a disease.
susceptible (suh-SEP-tuh-buhl) — Capable of being affected by something.
toxin (TOK-sin) — A poison that is produced by an organism (such as a plant, animal, or bacterium).

GLOSSARY

trailblazing (TREYL-bleyz-ing)—Making a way for others to follow.
tsetse fly (TSET-see FLAHY)—A fly found in Africa that feeds off the blood of humans and animals.
tsunami (tsoo-NAH-mee)—A large ocean wave that is produced by an earthquake of volcanic eruption under the ocean.
vaccine (vak-SEEN)—A substance that is put into the body to protect it against disease.
virus (VAHY-ruhs)—Genetic material surrounded by a coat of protein which creates copies of itself by using the cells of living hosts, and can often cause disease in the host.

INDEX

Access Campaign 32
Alex's Lemonade Stand 40, 42
Alzheimer's disease 34
American Cancer Society 14–18
American Red Cross 6–9, 10
aminopterin 14
asbestos 21, 38, 41
asbestosis 41
asthma 34, 36
Atkins Foundation 34, 35
Atkins, Robert and Veronica 34, 35
AVERT 29
bacteria 12, 13, 22, 41
Barton, Clara 6, 7, 8
Beckham, David 39
Brinker, Nancy 18–19
cancer 14–21, 29, 34, 42
 breast 18–20
 leukemia 14, 15, 17
Centers for Disease Control (CDC) 9, 27, 29
Chagas disease 30, 32
chemotherapy 14, 15, 17
childhood diseases 6, 9–12, 13, 14, 15, 17, 22, 26, 27, 33, 34, 37, 42
cholera 6, 30, 32–33
Civil War 6–8
communicable diseases 6, 9, 12, 22–28, 29, 30
congenital rubella syndrome 10
dengue fever 23
diabetes 34
diphtheria 6, 13
disaster relief 8–9, 30, 39
Easter Seals 26–27
Elton John AIDS Foundation 29
encephalitis 23
Doctors Without Borders 30–34
Farber, Sidney 15, 17
Gates, Bill and Melinda 11, 12

Gates Foundation 10–12, 13, 24, 27
GAVI Alliance 13
genetic diseases 17, 21, 41
Global Polio Eradication Initiative 27
Haiti 32–33
Harris, Paul P. 25
heart disease 21, 34
hepatitis B 13
HIV/AIDS 12, 29, 30
Hurricane Katrina 8–9
immune system 29, 37, 41
International AIDS Society 29
kala azar 30, 32
Komen, Susan 18, 19
lead 21, 38
malaria 12, 22–24, 30
Malaria No More 24
measles 6, 9–10, 11, 30
Measles and Rubella Initiative 9, 10
meningitis 13, 30, 33–34
Millenium Development Goals 11–12
mosquitoes 22, 23, 24
mumps 10
neglected diseases 32
Nigeria 10, 24
nutrition 5, 6, 18, 30, 31, 34, 35, 38, 41
obesity 34
Pakistan 10, 24
parasites 22, 30, 41
Peace Corps 22, 24
pertussis 13
Philippines 27, 39
pneumonia 6, 10, 13, 29
poliomyelitis 12, 24–27
PolioPlus 27
President's Malaria Initiative 24
prevention of disease 4, 5, 6, 10, 12, 13, 14, 17–18, 22–24, 25, 26, 27, 29, 32–34, 38, 41
Relay for Life 16, 17

research 5, 12, 14, 15, 17, 18, 19–20, 24, 25, 27, 34–36
rheumatoid arthritis 41
Rockefeller Foundation 27–28
Rockefeller, John D. 27–28
Rockefeller, John D. Jr. 28
Rockefeller University 27
Rotary Foundation 26–27
Rotary International 25–27
rubella 10
Salk, Jonas 26
Sandler Foundation 34, 36
Sandler, Herb and Marion 34
sanitation 5, 6, 38
sickle cell anemia 41
sleeping sickness 30, 32
smallpox 37
smoking 17, 18, 21, 38, 41
Stomp Out Malaria in Africa 24
Susan G. Komen for the Cure 18–20
Susan G. Komen Race for the Cure 18–19, 20
Switzerland 8, 29
tests, screening and diagnostic 6, 12, 17, 18, 24, 32–33
tetanus 13
Towards an HIV Cure 29
tuberculosis 12, 30
Typhoon Haiyan 39
United Kingdom 10, 29
United Nations 11
United Nations Children's Fund (UNICEF) 9, 13, 27, 39
vaccines 5, 6, 10, 11, 12, 13, 24, 25, 26, 27, 29, 32–34, 37, 38, 41
viruses 4, 9–10, 12, 13, 21, 22, 24, 29, 37, 41
volunteers 5, 8, 14, 20, 22, 24, 27, 40, 42
White, Ryan 29
World Health Organization (WHO) 9, 13, 22, 27, 37
yellow fever 13, 23

ABOUT THE AUTHOR

Marylou Morano Kjelle is a college English professor, freelance writer, and photojournalist who lives and works in Central New Jersey. Marylou has written dozens of books for young readers of all ages. She holds MS and MA degrees from Rutgers University, where she also teaches children's writing. When not teaching or writing, Marylou gardens, cooks, and bakes for her family and friends, watches movies, and reads as many books as she possibly can.